Godspeed, John Glenn

Godspeed,
John Glenn

Written and illustrated by Richard Hilliard

BOYDS MILLS PRESS

HONESDALE, PENNSYLVANIA

WHEN JOHN GLENN WAS A BOY living in Ohio, he and his dad took a ride in an airplane. This was a great thrill for young John, and he never forgot the feeling of flying through the sky. Many nights he lay in bed dreaming of flying planes when he grew up.

JOHN GLENN JR.

BORN: July 18, 1921, in Cambridge, Ohio

EDUCATION: Bachelor of science degree in engineering from Muskingum College; doctor of science degree (honorary) in engineering from Muskingum College.

HONORS AND MEDALS: Awarded the Distinguished Flying Cross on six occasions and holds the Air Medal with 18 Clusters for service during World War II and Korea. Also holds Navy Unit Commendation for service in Korea, the Asiatic-Pacific Campaign Medal, the American Campaign Medal, the World War II Victory Medal, the China Service Medal, the National Defense Service Medal, the Korean Service Medal, the United Nations Service Medal, the Korean Presidential Unit Citation, the Navy's Astronaut Wings, the Marine Corps' Astronaut Medal, the NASA Distinguished Service Medal, and the Congressional Space Medal of Honor.

In college, John studied aerodynamics and took flight classes. After the bombing of Pearl Harbor, John volunteered in the U.S. Navy. He became a fighter pilot in the Marine Corps and flew during both World War II and the war in Korea. He won many medals, including the Distinguished Flying Cross, the highest honor a pilot can receive.

As peacetime settled in the 1950s, John became a test pilot. Flying experimental aircraft, he went higher and faster with every flight. As America entered the "space age," John volunteered for a new and dangerous duty—becoming an astronaut.

It took a special breed of aviator to be a test pilot. Not only did the test pilot need to be an excellent flyer, but he also needed lightning-fast reflexes and the ability to think clearly under intense physical and emotional pressure. Making a critical decision a half second too late could mean disaster—and possibly death—when flying experimental aircraft. The men chosen for this hazardous duty were said by historians to have "the right stuff." In 1957 John Glenn became the first pilot to fly from New York to Los Angeles at supersonic speed (750 mph or faster). He made the flight in 3 hours and 23 minutes.

Each man was a highly trained aviator, but training to go into space required the toughest physical and mental conditioning they had ever seen. This was partly due to the unknown factors of performing in the weightlessness of space, but also because the whole world would be watching them taking these first steps. The slightest error could spell disaster for not only the astronaut but also the future of America's space program. For the astronauts, perfection was the only option.

Hundreds of men tested for this new service that would ultimately launch Americans into the vacuum of space. In 1959 John Glenn was selected along with six other test pilots to become America's first astronauts—the Mercury Seven. John didn't know where the Astronaut Corps would take him, but he was excited to be one of the first pioneers of this new frontier.

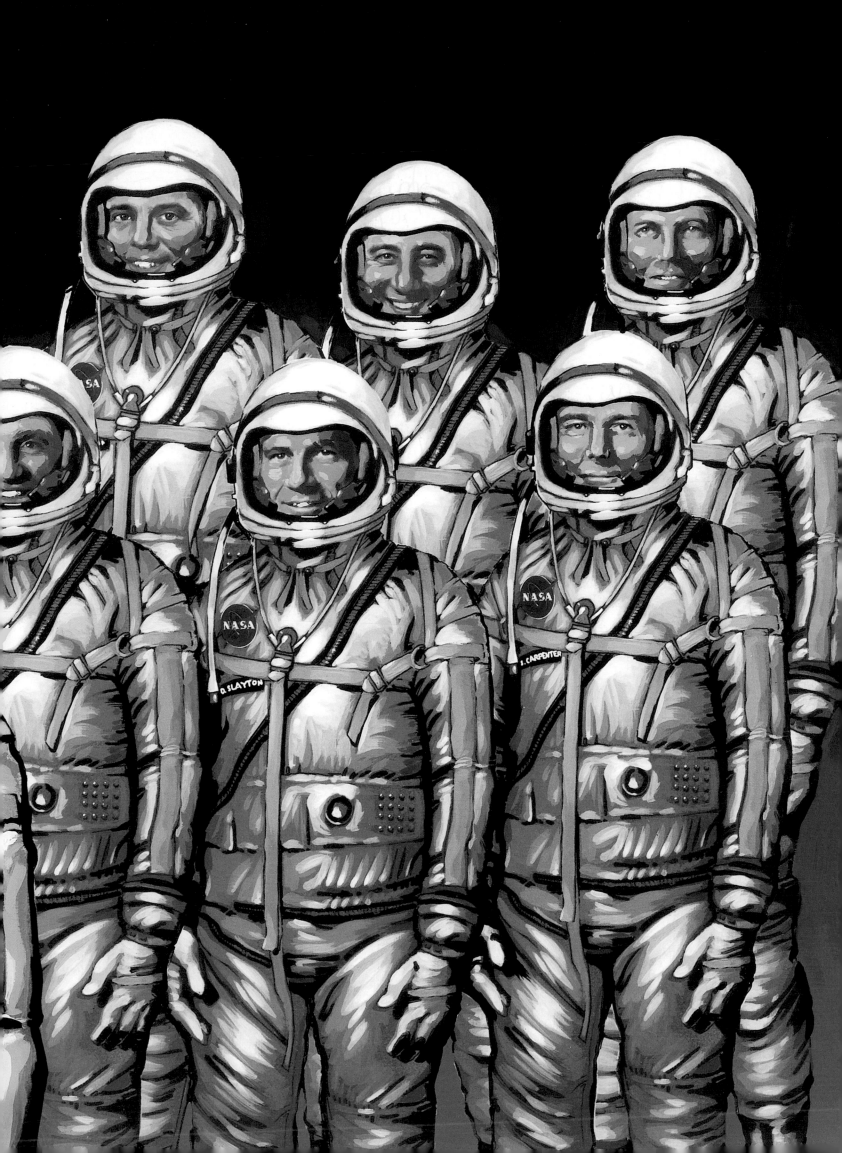

As the astronauts spent many months in training, America began to send chimpanzees into space. People started to wonder if the astronauts were up to the difficult challenge of going into orbit. John and the others knew they were ready but needed to make sure the spacecraft was safe enough to take a man into space and bring him back to Earth.

Before men and women ventured into orbit, rockets carried animals into the sky. This tested whether a living creature could withstand the changes in pressure and be brought back to Earth without injury. America's first space celebrity was Ham. This male chimpanzee flew into space on January 31, 1961, blasting off from Cape Canaveral and traveling more than 150 miles in a Mercury capsule before splashing down safely in the ocean. His little pod was strapped into the human-sized seat, providing him with oxygen and keeping him comfortable. Ham became famous after the flight and was featured on many magazine covers.

For the first two American space flights, the capsules rode atop small Redstone boosters into suborbital space. The Redstone was not powerful enough to push the Mercury capsule into orbit. To get the needed power for orbit, American rocket scientists turned to the Atlas booster rocket for their next flight. Unfortunately, the Atlas had many failed test launches, which caused the big rocket to explode. Scientists worked night and day to fix the problem. The Atlas was finally ready to fly with the third manned mission that would take John Glenn into space. The rocket consisted of three main parts: the escape tower, which would carry the capsule away from the booster in an emergency; the capsule, which held the astronaut and instrumentation; and the booster, which carried the main fuel and rocket engines.

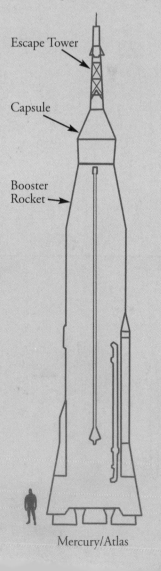

Escape Tower

Capsule

Booster
Rocket →

Mercury/Atlas

The first missions to carry astronauts into orbit were called Mercury. The first two human missions went only to the edge of space, proving an astronaut could work in the weightless environment. The third mission would send an astronaut into orbit around Earth, circling the planet many times. John felt very honored when he was selected to take this historic flight.

On February 20, 1962, on a launch platform at Cape Canaveral, Florida, John was strapped into the small Mercury capsule, called *Friendship 7*. As the countdown ended, the giant Atlas rocket engine roared to life, slowly raising the spacecraft off the launch platform. As John's capsule cleared the tower, astronaut Scott Carpenter radioed the world, "Godspeed, John Glenn," wishing him good luck as he rose into the sky.

Once the Atlas booster was out of fuel, it separated from the capsule, falling back to Earth. This is called "staging." A booster rocket's fate depends on its size. A booster may fall through the atmosphere, building up heat and burning up before it gets anywhere near the surface. If it is so large that it could not burn up entirely, parachutes would bring it back for a soft ocean landing. The Atlas was not large enough to need an ocean landing, so it burned up once it came back into Earth's atmosphere. Having done its job of putting the capsule into orbit, it was no longer needed.

As the Atlas booster fell back to Earth, *Friendship 7* was pushed into orbit. For the first time in his life, John saw the curve of the earth glowing brightly in the inky blackness of space. The stars looked brighter than he had ever seen them before, and the Moon looked close enough to touch. As his capsule orbited into the dark, he saw lights on the land far below him. John exclaimed, "It's a beautiful sight!"

Everything was going perfectly, and John was told by Mission Control that he could expect at least seven orbits of the globe, each orbit taking only eighty-eight minutes. Although the *Friendship 7* capsule was very cramped, John felt comfortable in the weightless environment as he conducted experiments and piloted the capsule around the world. From every corner of the globe, people tuned in their radios and televisions to hear the updates on John's flight.

Although the Mercury astronauts were in one-man capsules traveling through space, they were never truly alone. Back on Earth, the people of Mission Control constantly monitored them. Linked to the capsule by radio signals, the technicians could keep track of almost every function of the spacecraft in orbit. Doctors were able to watch the astronaut's heartbeat and breathing patterns, while engineers monitored the speed and location of the capsule. If anything went wrong, Mission Control was there to help the astronaut work through the problem.

Like a giant bowl covering the bottom of the space capsule, the heat shield protected the spacecraft from burning up during reentry. Made of thick, ceramic material, the heat shield absorbed and deflected the temperature buildup as the capsule plunged through Earth's upper atmosphere. As the capsule fell, air molecules moved against the surface, creating friction. This friction gets so intense that the bottom of the capsule turns into a fireball. Without the heat shield, the capsule could never return safely.

UNITED STATES

Friendship 7

Back at Mission Control in Florida, things looked good until suddenly a beeping alarm sounded, indicating something was wrong. The heat shield on John's capsule might be loose, and if it came off, John would burn up as the spacecraft reentered Earth's atmosphere. Everyone decided that John would have to be brought back after only three orbits.

As the capsule plunged back to Earth, John's spacecraft was engulfed in flame. His only protection was the heat shield that might not be working properly, and the retropack, which began to melt and break away from the bottom of the capsule. Everyone at Mission Control was nervous that John would not return safely. Even John was worried and started humming a tune to himself to stay calm. Hearing John's voice through the crackling radio, Mission Control knew he survived the fiery descent. He radioed to Scott and the others at the Cape, "That was a real fireball there!"

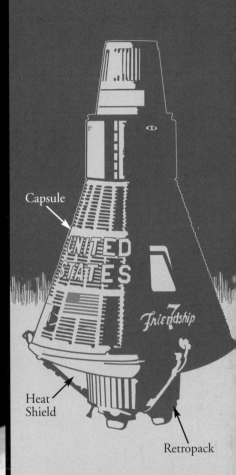

Capsule

Heat
Shield

Retropack

With the possibility of a loose heat shield, Mission Control decided to leave the retropack attached to the bottom of John's capsule. Normally, this small collection of rocket nozzles would be jettisoned, or automatically pushed away before reentry. Mission Control hoped the pack's straps would hold the heat shield in place. As it later turned out, the malfunction was not with the heat shield but with the control panel on Earth. In any event, fast thinking helped maintain the astronaut's safety.

Almost two miles above the waters of the Pacific Ocean, a big parachute shot out of the capsule's nose as the flames died down. *Friendship 7* floated gently into the waves as U.S. Navy ships moved in to pick up John and his capsule. The navy crew cheered wildly for John as he came aboard the large ship.

John F. Kennedy was the president of the United States during the early days of the space program. After the first successful Mercury mission in 1961, Kennedy became convinced that landing on the Moon could be achieved by American astronauts. He set a goal for NASA and the rest of the country to get a man on the Moon by the end of 1969. Many did not believe this was possible, but President Kennedy, as America's foremost space cheerleader of the day, did everything he could to make this dream a reality. John Glenn's successful mission was a major step in realizing Kennedy's dream.

After the historic flight, John became a hero to millions of people around the world who were inspired by his courage in facing the unknown. Huge crowds lined the streets of Washington, D.C., as a parade took John and his wife, Annie, to meet the president. Later John gave a speech to Congress about the importance of space exploration and the quest to land on the Moon.

John left the Astronaut Corps and Marines in 1964 and later became a prominent U.S. senator. In 1998, he surprised the world when he went back into space aboard the space shuttle *Discovery*. Now a grandfather, John Glenn is living proof that life's adventures never stop.

For Vincent Di Fate

Special thanks to

*John and Annie Glenn; Joyce Burns of the Smithsonian Institution;
Roger D. Launius, Ph.D., chair, Division of Space History, Smithsonian National Air and Space Museum;
Ted and Betsy Lewin; Murray Tinkelman; and Adrienne*

Text and illustrations copyright © 2006 by Richard Hilliard
All rights reserved

Boyds Mills Press, Inc.
A Highlights Company
815 Church Street
Honesdale, Pennsylvania 18431
Printed in China

Library of Congress Cataloging-in-Publication Data

Hilliard, Richard.
Godspeed, John Glenn / written and illustrated by Richard Hilliard.
p. cm.
ISBN-13: 978-1-59078-384-9 (hardcover : alk. paper)
1. Glenn, John, 1921—Juvenile literature. 2. Astronauts—United States—Biography—Juvenile literature.
3. Legislators—United States—Biography—Juvenile literature. I. Title.

TL789.85.G6H55 2006
629.450092—dc22

2006000517

First edition, 2006
The text of this book is set in 16-point Garamond.
The illustrations are done in acrylic.

Visit our Web site at www.boydsmillspress.com

10 9 8 7 6 5 4 3 2 1